Alfred's

Music for Little Mozarts

The *Rhythm Speller Book 3* reinforces rhythm skills based on the concepts introduced in the *Music Lesson Book 3*. The pages in the book correlate page by page with the materials in the *Music Lesson Book*. They should be assigned according to the instructions in the upper right corner of the pages in this book. They may also be assigned as review material at any time after the students have passed the designated *Music Lesson Book* page.

Each page of the *Rhythm Speller Book* has two activities—a **rhythm-writing** activity and a **rhythm-reading** activity. The written activities reinforce note values and counting through coloring, circling, drawing, or matching. The rhythm-reading activities help students practice:

• Clapping or tapping rhythm patterns while counting aloud.

• Playing rhythms on rhythm instruments or keys on the keyboard. (Other rhythm instruments can be substituted for those suggested throughout the book.)

• Chanting words based on rhythm patterns.

Alfred Music
P.O. Box 10003
Van Nuys, CA 91410-0003
alfred.com

Copyright © 2018 by Alfred Music
All rights reserved. Printed in USA.

No part of this book shall be reproduced, arranged, adapted, recorded, publicly performed, stored in a retrieval system, or transmitted by any means without written permission from the publisher. In order to comply with copyright laws, please apply for such written permission and/or license by contacting the publisher at alfred.com/permissions.

ISBN-10: 1-4706-4052-X
ISBN-13: 978-1-4706-4052-1

Illustrations by Christine Finn

Christine H. Barden · Gayle Kowalchyk · E. L. Lancaster

Use with Alfred's Music for Little Mozarts,
Lesson Book 3, page 5.

Rhythm Writing

Draw a line connecting the dots to match the rhythm patterns to their counts.

Rhythm Reading

Clap the *Professor Haydn Hippo* rhythm pattern and chant the words.

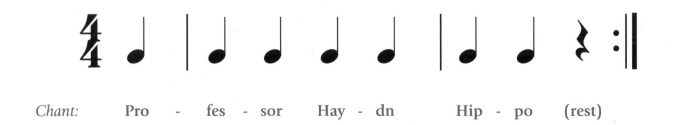

Chant: Pro - fes - sor   Hay - dn   Hip - po   (rest)

Rhythm Writing

Draw a line connecting the dots to match each rhythm pattern to its correct time signature.

Rhythm Reading

Tap the rhythm pattern on your lap. Tap notes with an up stem (𝅗𝅥.) with your RH.

Tap notes with a down stem (𝅘𝅥) with your LH. Count aloud.

Count: 1 - 2 - 3   1 - 2 - 3   1   1   1   1 - 2 - 3

Use with page 7.

Rhythm Writing

Draw a line connecting the dots to match the rhythm patterns to their counts.

   •   •   **1 rest 1 rest | 1 1 1 rest**

   •   •   **1 - 2 1 - 2 | 1 1 1 rest**

   •   •   **1 1 1 1 | 1 1 1 rest**

Rhythm Reading

 Using finger 3 of the RH, play the rhythm pattern on  and count aloud.

Count: 1 - 2 - 3   1 - 2 - 3   1   1   1   1 - 2 - 3

 Using finger 2 of the LH, play the rhythm pattern on 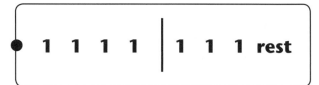 and count aloud.

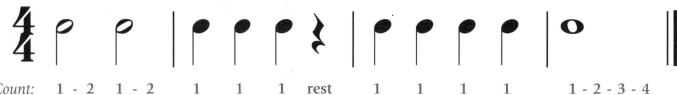

Count: 1 - 2   1 - 2   1   1   1   rest   1   1   1   1   1 - 2 - 3 - 4

Rhythm Writing

Draw a **dotted half note** in each blank measure.

Then, clap and count the rhythm pattern.

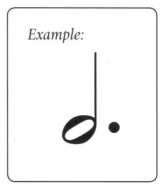

Example:

Rhythm Reading

Clap the *Nannerl Mouse* rhythm pattern and chant the words.

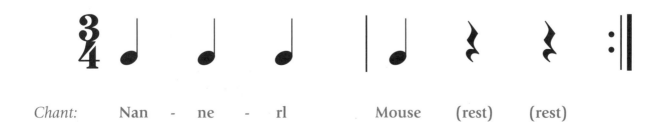

Chant: Nan   –   ne   –   rl   Mouse   (rest)   (rest)

Use with page 11.

Rhythm Writing

1. Circle the rhythm pattern  with a **blue** crayon.

2. Circle the rhythm pattern with an **orange** crayon.

3. Circle the rhythm pattern  with a **gray** crayon.

Rhythm Reading

1. Clap and tap the rhythm pattern. Clap notes with an up stem (♩).
   Tap notes with a down stem (♩) on your lap. Count aloud.

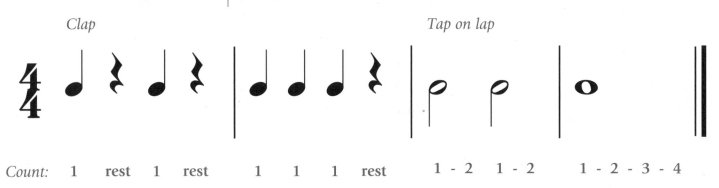

Clap   *Tap on lap*

Count: 1   rest   1   rest   1   1   1   rest   1 - 2   1 - 2   1 - 2 - 3 - 4

2. Using finger 2 of the LH, play the above rhythm pattern on
   Then, play again with LH finger 3.

Rhythm Writing

1. Change each **whole note** to a **quarter note** by coloring it **black** and drawing a stem on the right.

2. Change each **half note** to a **dotted half note** by adding a dot on the right.

3. Then, clap and count the rhythm.

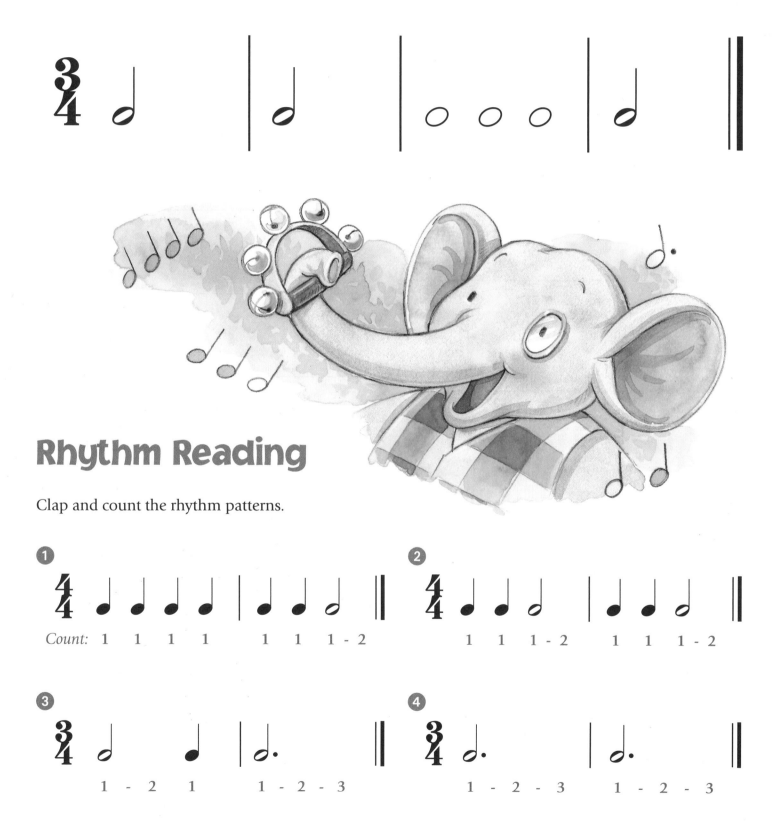

Rhythm Reading

Clap and count the rhythm patterns.

1.

$\frac{4}{4}$

Count: 1   1   1   1   1   1   1 - 2

2.

$\frac{4}{4}$

1   1   1 - 2   1   1   1 - 2

3.

$\frac{3}{4}$

1 - 2   1   1 - 2 - 3

4.

$\frac{3}{4}$

1 - 2 - 3   1 - 2 - 3

5. Play each rhythm pattern (1–4) with bells.

Use with page 15.

Rhythm Writing

Draw a line connecting the dots to match the rhythm patterns to their counts.

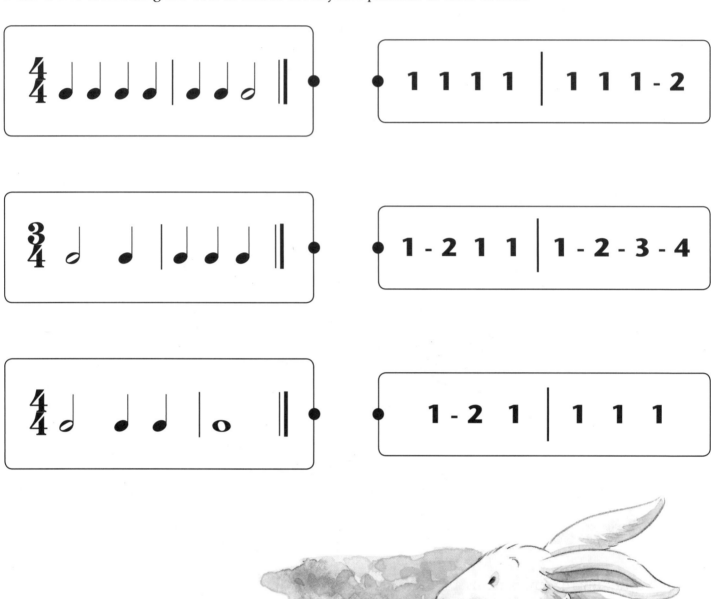

Rhythm Reading

Tap the rhythm pattern on your lap. Tap notes with a down stem (♩) with your LH.

Tap notes with an up stem (♩) with your RH. Count aloud.

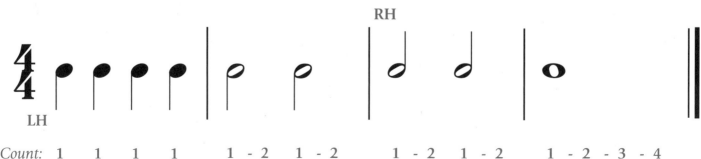

Count: 1   1   1   1   1 - 2   1 - 2   1 - 2   1 - 2   1 - 2 - 3 - 4

Rhythm Writing

Draw a **quarter note** in each box.

Then, clap and count the rhythm patterns.

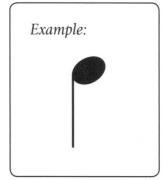
Example:

  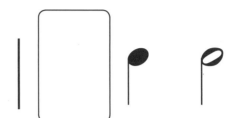

 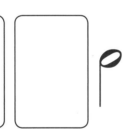  

Rhythm Reading

Clap and count the rhythm patterns.

Count: 1   rest   1   rest   1 - 2 - 3 - 4

1   1   1   1   1 - 2   1 - 2

1   1   1   1   1   1   1   rest

1 - 2   1 - 2   1   1   1 - 2

5 Play each rhythm pattern (1–4) on a wood block.

Use with page 19.

Rhythm Writing

Circle each rhythm pattern in **¾** time.

Draw a line through each rhythm pattern in **4/4** time.

Rhythm Reading

1 Clap and tap the rhythm pattern. Tap notes with a down stem ( ) on your lap.

Clap notes with an up stem ( ). Count aloud.

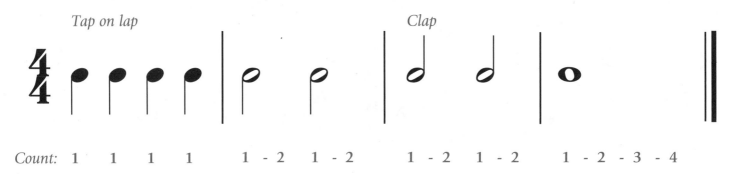

2 Play the above rhythm pattern with a tambourine.

Rhythm Writing

Draw a **dotted half note** in each blank measure.

Then, clap and count the rhythm patterns.

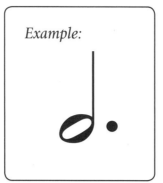

Example:

Rhythm Reading

Clap and count the rhythm patterns.

1

Count: 1 - 2   1   1 - 2 - 3

2

1   1   1   1 - 2 - 3

3

1   1   1 rest   1   1   1 rest

4

1   1   1   1   1 - 2 - 3 - 4

5 Play each rhythm pattern (1–4) with rhythm sticks.

Use with page 23.

Rhythm Writing

Draw a line connecting the dots to match the rhythm patterns to their counts.

$\frac{3}{4}$ ♩. | ♩. | ♩ ♩ | ♩. ‖ •	• **1 1 1 | 1 1 1 | 1-2 1-2**
$\frac{4}{4}$ ♩ ♩ ♩ | ♩ ♩ ♩ ♩ | ♩ ♩ ‖ •	• **1 1 1-2 | 1 1 1 1 | 1-2 1-2**
$\frac{4}{4}$ ♩ ♩ ♩ ♩ | ♩ ♩ ♩ ♩ | ♩ ♩ ‖ •	• **1-2-3 | 1-2-3 | 1-2 1 | 1-2-3**

Rhythm Reading

Play each rhythm pattern with rhythm sticks. Count aloud.

1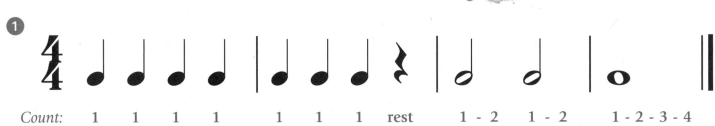

Count: 1   1   1   1   1   1   1   rest   1 - 2   1 - 2   1 - 2 - 3 - 4

2

Count: 1 - 2 - 3   1 - 2 - 3   1 - 2   1   1 - 2 - 3

Rhythm Writing

Draw a line connecting the dots to match each rhythm pattern to its correct time signature.

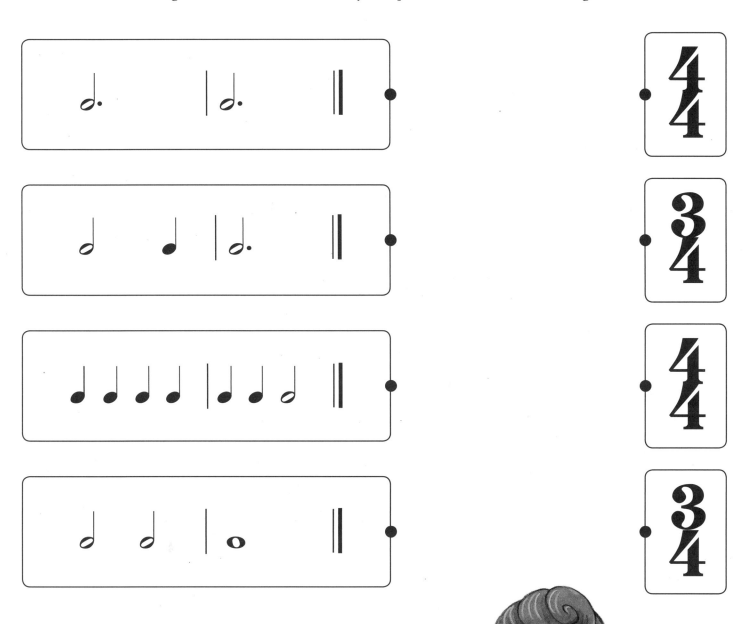

Rhythm Reading

Clap the *Nina Ballerina* rhythm pattern and chant the words.

Chant: Ni - na   Bal - le - ri - na

Use with page 27.

Rhythm Writing

1 Circle each rest that gets one count.

2 Draw an **X** through each rest that gets two counts.

Rhythm Reading

Clap and count the rhythm patterns.

1

$\frac{4}{4}$ ♩ ♩ ♩ ♩ | 𝅗𝅥 ♩ 𝄾 ‖

Count: 1   1   1   1   1 - 2   1   rest

2

$\frac{4}{4}$ ♩ ♩ ♩ ♩ | 𝅗𝅥 – ‖

1   1   1   1   1 - 2   rest - 2

3

$\frac{3}{4}$ ♩ ♩ ♩ | 𝅗𝅥 𝄾 ‖

1   1   1   1 - 2   rest

4

$\frac{3}{4}$ 𝅗𝅥 ♩ | 𝅗𝅥. ‖

1 - 2   1   1 - 2 - 3

5 Play each rhythm pattern (1–4) with bells.

Rhythm Writing

Draw a line connecting the dots to match the rhythm patterns to their counts.

1 1 1 | 1 - 2 rest

1 - 2 1 - 2 | 1 - 2 1 - 2

1 1 1 1 | 1 - 2 rest - 2

Rhythm Reading

Tap the rhythm pattern on your lap. Tap notes with a down stem (♩) with your LH.

Tap notes with an up stem (♩) with your RH. Count aloud.

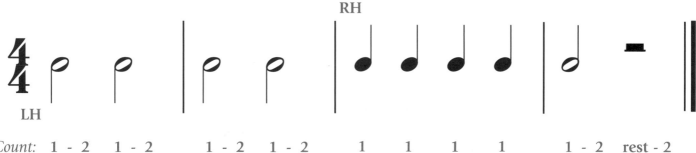

Count: 1 - 2   1 - 2   1 - 2   1 - 2   1   1   1   1   1 - 2   rest - 2

Use with page 31.

Rhythm Writing

Clap the rhythm patterns. Then, draw a line to match each rhythm pattern to the music friend whose name matches the rhythm.

Pro-fes-sor Hay-dn Hip-po

nan-ne-rl Mouse

Bee-tho-ven Bear

Rhythm Reading

1 Clap and tap the rhythm pattern. Tap notes with a down stem (♩) on your lap.

Clap notes with an up stem (♩). Count aloud.

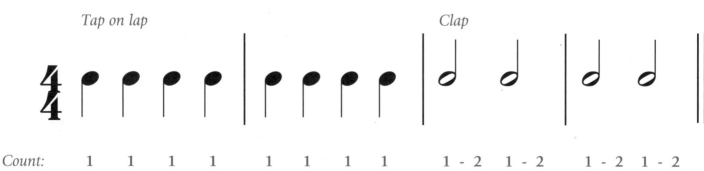

Tap on lap   *Clap*

Count: 1   1   1   1   1   1   1   1   1 - 2   1 - 2   1 - 2   1 - 2

2 Using finger 1 of the LH, play the above rhythm pattern on Then, play again with LH finger 2.

Rhythm Writing

Draw a **half note** in each box.

Then, clap and count the rhythm patterns.

Example:

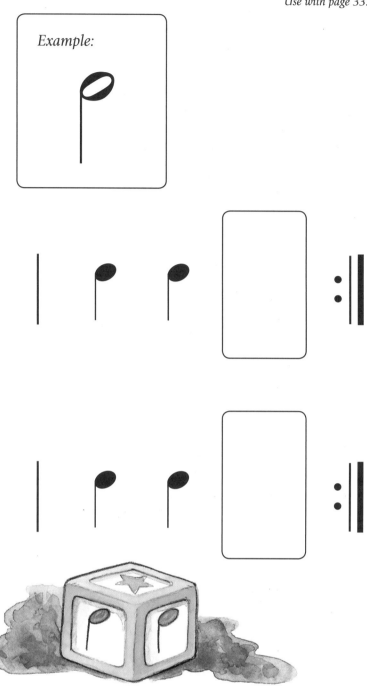

Rhythm Reading

Clap and count the rhythm patterns.

①
Count: 1   1   1   1   1   1

②
1   1   1   1 - 2 - 3

③
1   1   1 - 2   1 - 2   1 - 2

④
1   1   1 - 2   1 - 2 - 3 - 4

⑤ Play each rhythm pattern (1–4) on a wood block.

Use with page 35.

Rhythm Writing

Draw a line connecting the dots to match the rhythm patterns to their counts.

Rhythm Reading

1 Using finger 2 of the RH, play the rhythm pattern on and count aloud.

Count: 1 - 2   1   1 - 2   1   1 - 2 - 3   1 - 2 - 3

2 Using finger 2 of the LH, play the rhythm pattern on and count aloud.

Count: 1   1   1   rest   1 - 2 - 3   rest   1   1   1   rest   1 - 2 - 3   rest

Rhythm Writing

Circle each rhythm pattern in **¾** time.

Draw a line through each rhythm pattern in **4/4** time.

Rhythm Reading

Clap and count the rhythm patterns.

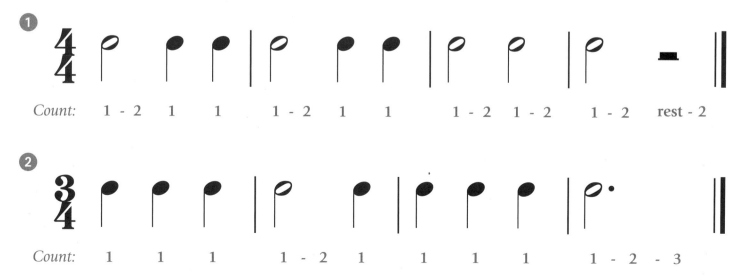

1

Count: 1 - 2   1   1   1 - 2   1   1   1 - 2   1 - 2   1 - 2   rest - 2

2

Count: 1   1   1   1 - 2   1   1   1   1   1   1 - 2 - 3

Use with page 39.

Rhythm Writing

Draw a **half note** and two **quarter notes** in each blank measure.

Then, clap and count the rhythm pattern.

Example:

Rhythm Reading

1 Clap and tap the rhythm patterns. Clap notes with an up stem (♩).
Tap notes with a down stem (↑) on your lap. Count aloud.

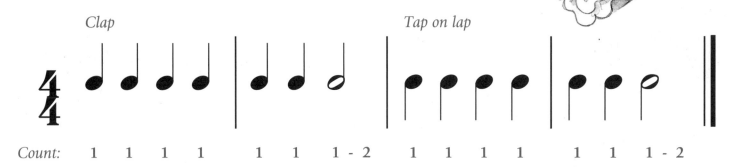

Clap   *Tap on lap*

Count: 1   1   1   1   1   1   1 - 2   1   1   1   1   1   1   1 - 2

2

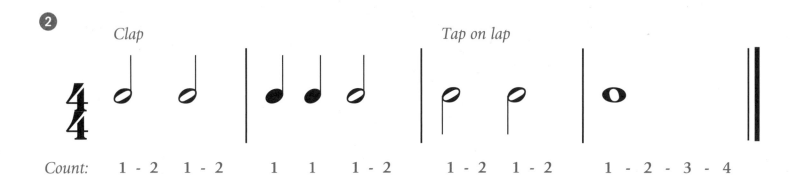

Clap   *Tap on lap*

Count: 1 - 2   1 - 2   1   1   1 - 2   1 - 2   1 - 2   1 - 2 - 3 - 4

3 Play the above rhythm patterns with rhythm sticks.

Rhythm Writing

Draw a line connecting the dots to match the rhythm patterns to their counts.

1 1 1 | 1 1 1-2 | 1 1 1-2

1 1 1 | 1 - 2 1 | 1 - 2 - 3

1 1 1 | 1 - 2 - 3 | 1 - 2 - 3

Rhythm Reading

Play each rhythm pattern with rhythm sticks. Count aloud.

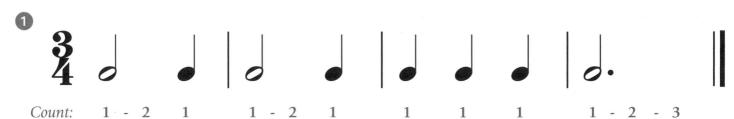

Count: 1 - 2   1   1 - 2   1   1   1   1   1 - 2 - 3

Count: 1   1   1   1 - 2 - 3   1   1   1   1 - 2 - 3

Use with page 43.

Rhythm Writing

Draw a **dotted half note** in each blank measure.

Then, clap and count the rhythm patterns.

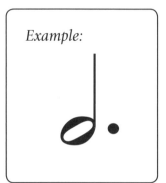

Example:

Rhythm Reading

Clap and count the rhythm patterns.

①

Count: 1 - 2   1   1 - 2 - 3

②

1 - 2 - 3   1 - 2 - 3

③

1   1   1 - 2   1 - 2   1 - 2

④

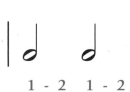  

1   1   1   1   1   1   1 - 2

⑤ Play each rhythm pattern (1–4) on a tambourine.

Rhythm Writing

Draw a line connecting the dots to match each rhythm pattern to its correct time signature.

Rhythm Reading

Tap the rhythm pattern on your lap. Tap notes with an up stem (♩) with your RH.

Tap notes with a down stem (♩) with your LH. Count aloud.

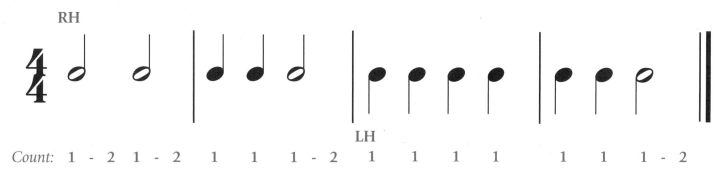

Count: 1 - 2   1 - 2   1   1   1 - 2   1   1   1   1   1   1   1 - 2

Use with page 47.

Rhythm Writing

Draw two **quarter notes** and a **half note** in each blank measure.

Then, clap and count the rhythm pattern.

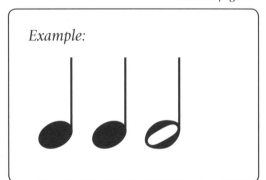

Example:

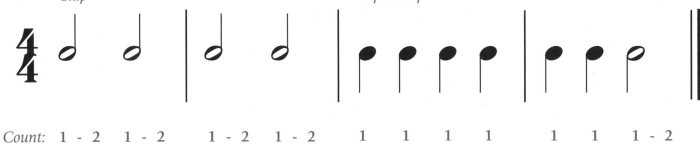

Rhythm Reading

1 Clap and tap the rhythm pattern. Clap notes with an up stem (♩).
Tap notes with a down stem (♩) on your lap. Count aloud.

Clap   *Tap on lap*

Count: 1 - 2   1 - 2   1 - 2   1 - 2   1   1   1   1   1   1   1 - 2

2 Play the above rhythm pattern with rhythm sticks.